W9-CHD-535

Essential Question
How does your body move?

We Can Move!

by Mateo Garza

Our bodies have many parts.
The parts help us move.

We move all day. We move a lot when we play sports!

We move to play baseball.
Our arms and hands help.
We swing a bat. We catch
and throw a ball.

Our legs and feet help.
We run around the bases.

We move when we play soccer. We stop and turn quickly.

We have to be fast. Our feet move to kick the ball.

We move when we swim.
Our two arms and hands
help us.

Our legs help, too. We jump into the pool. We kick and push the water.

We move when we tumble.
Our arms help us go
upside down!

We also move in other ways. How do you move?

Respond to Reading

Retell

Use your own words to retell details in *We Can Move!*

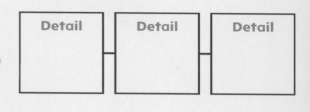

Text Evidence

1. Look at page 4. What details tell how you move when you play baseball? Key Details

2. Look at pages 5 and 9. What can legs help you do? Key Details

3. How do you know that *We Can Move!* is nonfiction? Genre

Compare Texts
What helps you move?

What's Under Your Skin?

Do you know what's under your skin?

Under your skin, you have a skeleton. Your skeleton is made of bones. They help hold you up. They help you move, too. When your bones grow, you get taller!

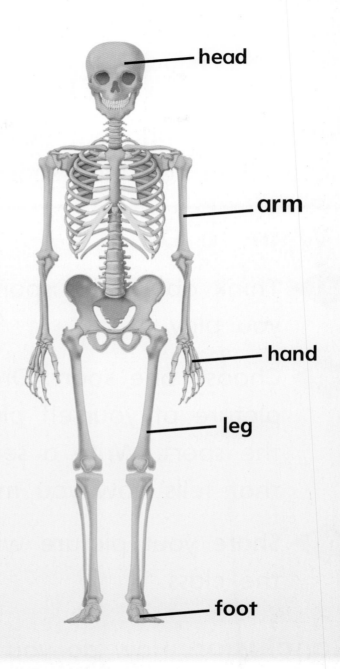

head

arm

hand

leg

foot

Make Connections
Look at both selections. How does your body move? Text to Text

Focus on
Science

Purpose To find out how you move when you play sports

What to Do

Step 1 ▶ Think about the sports you play.

Step 2 ▶ Choose one sport. Draw a picture of yourself playing the sport. Write a sentence that tells how you move.

Step 3 ▶ Share your picture with the class.

Conclusion How do you move when you play sports?